SCIFAIKUEST

February 2025

*

THE STAFF OF SCIFAIKUEST:
TERI SANTITORO, EDITOR

SCIFAIKUEST is published quarterly online and in print. The two editions are different.

Cover art "Persephone" by Richard E. Schell
Cover design by Laura Givens

Vol. XXII, No. 3 February 2025
Scifaikuest [ISSN 1558-9730] is published quarterly on the 1st day of February, May, August, and November in the United States of America by Hiraeth Publishing, P.O. Box 1248, Tularosa, NM 88352. Any similarity between places and persons mentioned in the fiction or semi-fiction and real places or persons living or dead is coincidental. Writers and artists guidelines are available online at https://www.hiraethsffh.com/scifaikuest. Guidelines are also available upon request from Hiraeth Publishing, P.O. Box 1248, Tularosa, NM, 88352, if request is accompanied by a SASE #10 envelope with a first-class US stamp. Subscriptions: $28 for one year [4 issues], $44 for two years [8 issues]. Single copies $9.00 postage paid in the United States. Subscriptions to Canada: $33 for one year, $51 for two years. Single copies $11.00 postage paid to Canada. U.S. and Canadian subscribers remit in U.S. funds. All other countries inquire about rates.

What???
No subscription to
Scifaikuest??

We can fix that . . .

https://www.hiraethsffh.com/product-page/scifaikuest-1

Or get a sample back issue to check us out!

https://www.hiraethsffh.com/shop-1

And a subscription makes a great gift, for a holiday or any time of the year!

Minimalism:

A Handbook of Minimalist Genre Poetic Forms

MINIMALISM
A Handbook of Minimalist Genre Poetic Forms
Edited by Teri Santitoro

This handbook contains articles about how to write various minimalist poetry forms such as scifaiku, senryu, sijo, haibun, empat perkataan, ghazals, cinquain, cherita, rengays, rengu, octains, tanka, threesomes, and many more. Each article is written by an expert in that particular poetry form.

Teri Santitoro, aka sakyu, who assembled this handbook, has been the editor of Scifaikuest since 2003.

https://www.hiraethsffh.com/product-page/minimalism-a-handbook-of-minimalist-genre-poetic-forms

A Little Help, Please

In the world of the small indie press we fight a never-ending battle for attention to our work, as writers and in publishing. Here's an example: big publishers [you know who they are] have gobs of $$ $ that they can devote to advertising and marketing. Here at Hiraeth Publishing, our advertising budget consists of the deposits for whatever soda bottles and aluminum cans we can find alongside the highways. Anti-littering laws make our task even more difficult . . . ☺

That's where YOU come in. YOU are our best promoter. YOU are the one who can tell others about us. Just send 'em to our website, tell them about our store. That's all. Just that.

Of course, we don't mind if you talk us up. We're pretty good, you know. We have some award-winning and award-nominated writers and artists, plus other voices well-deserving to be heard [not everyone wins awards, right?] but our publications are read-worthy nevertheless.

That number once again is:

www.hiraethsffh.com

Friend us on Facebook at Hiraeth Publishing

Follow us on Twitter at @HiraethPublish1

SALE!!

There's a sale going on!! It's still going on!!

All the books you can order at 20% off the total! Woot!

Buy 1 book; buy 100 books! It's all the same discount. Use the code **BOOKS2025** when you check out.

Go to the Shop at www.hiraethsffh.com and make those selections now!

You'll be glad you did. So will we.

Aliens, Magic, and Monsters
By Lauren McBride

A SPECULATIVE COLLECTION
ALIENS, MAGIC, AND MONSTERS
BY LAUREN McBRIDE

Fun to read. Fun to write. *Aliens, Magic, and Monsters* features poems set in the unlimited and imaginative realm of science fiction, fantasy, and horror. The poems were chosen to showcase over twenty poetic forms from acrostiku to zip, from strict rhyme to free verse, and much more in between. There are guidelines included on how to write each type of poem. Try a sci(na)ku. At only six words, it's sure to interest even the youngest readers.

Type: Juvenile and Young Adult Poetry Manual

Ordering links:
Print: https://www.hiraethsffh.com/product-page/aliens-magic-and-monsters-by-lauren-mcbride

ePub: https://www.hiraethsffh.com/product-page/aliens-magic-and-monsters-by-lauren-mcbride-2

PDF: https://www.hiraethsffh.com/product-page/aliens-magic-and-monsters-by-lauren-mcbride-1

Greetings and Happy Valentine's Day!

We have some *really* excellent poetry in this issue, and I can't wait to share it with you!

In this edition we are very fortunate to also have a wonderful article by RE Porter, which I hope you will enjoy. Our Featured Poet this issue is Royal Baysinger and you won't want to miss his thoughtful and insightful poems.

Once again we are also blessed to have a great variety of illustrations by both Lisa Timpf and Richard E Schell, who did our gorgeous cover, *"Persephone"*, as well!

All in all, this is an awesome issue, full of everything we love. So kick back, get comfortable and immerse yourself!

Scifaikuest now has its own ISBN!!! Please inform your local book stores and library that they are now able to ORDER SCIFAIKUEST!!!

You can now find us at Hiraeth Books at:
https://www.hiraethsffh.com/home-1

If you don't have a subscription to our PRINT edition, they are available at:
https://www.hiraethsffh.com/product-page/scifaikuest

And, if you would like to join the select group of contributors by submitting your poetry, artwork or article, you can find our guidelines at:
https://www.hiraethsffh.com/scifaikuest

You can also read our ONLINE VERSION at:
https://www.hiraethsffh.com/scifaikuest-online

Pssst! Looking for something good to read?
You can get t.santitoro's newest book, The Red Foil, a SF mystery, at:
https://www.hiraethsffh.com/product-page/red-foil-by-t-santitoro

and you can find her novella, *Those Who Die,* at:
THOSE WHO DIE by t. santitoro | Hiraeth Publishing (hiraethsffh.com)

You can also order t.santitoro's novella, *Adopted Child*, at:
https://www.hiraethsffh.com/product-page/adopted-child-by-t-santitoro

And you can still get a copy of her vampire novelette, *The Legend of Trey Valentine*, at:
https://www.hiraethsffh.com/product-page/legend-of-trey-valentine-by-teri-santitoro

As always, I'd love to extend a huge Scifaikuest Welcome to our newest contributors: Elaine Dillof, Douglas J. Lanzo, Geoffrey Reiter, and Joy Yin!

t. rex dreams
futuristic hunt
searching for dachshunds

Scifaiku and Illustration by Richard E. Schell

The Richard E. Schell Page

sacrifices endured
fortune's celebration
mars first born

volcanoes of io
unimaginably inhospitable
unless you're born there

earthshaking roar
fire pierces the fog
starship leaves for mars

I reach out
unexpectedly a tentacle
touches yours

The Greg Schwartz Page

funeral...
the robot offers her
a tissue

orbiting Saturn he proposes

house hunting
two-story colonial
with a view of Olympus Mons

queen of hearts
another severed head
on the pile

The Geetanjali Lachke Page

Mars' rusty landscape
rovers in search of life forms
red dust in the wind

interstellar winds
carrying a distant ditty
an alien song

black orbs zooming in
so unlike our pretty eyes
alien beauty

The Gary Davis Page

Bob launched time machine
spins dizzy through dark space
bounced off Big Bang

deep diving subs
may float among clouds
Venus awaits

Captain Jill Earthbound
global pathogen unleashed
virus of Venus

Far-Fetched Future of Space Flight

spaceport swimming pool
lost spin gravity
swimmers drown mid-air

The DJ Tyrer Page

secret kisses
late-night seduction
bloodsucker

coffin lid rises
I watch trembling
stake in hand

haunted house
reassuring hand holds mine
I'm alone

The John H. Dromey Page

enchanted forest
elves resent mushroom pickers
shoplifting toadstools

Re: Orion's Belt
universe is expanding
switched to suspenders

meat from Planet X
don't say it tastes like chicken
just because it's foul

tourist tidal wave
with lunar destination
full moon

The Benjamin Whitney Norris Page

golfers staked out

golfers staked out
on the shooting range
a hole in one

reboot

sweeping away
the mental cobwebs
blank slate again

one night stand

from the night before last
a torn lung bleeding
on my doorstop

no apple for Yvonne

on her desk
a shrunken head
the teacher's "pet"

SCIFAIKU

a vacuum-sealed room
karaoke machine crammed
with old earth standards

William Shaw

gnarled olive tree
memories of Romans
flowing through old veins

Douglas J. Lanzo

ghost dog
fetches a bone
master's grave

Miguel O. Mitchell

robot cat
ignores when called
perfect replica

Miguel O. Mitchell

the plunger sinks
torpor spreads beneath his skin
with dreams of her

Christina Nordlander

PSA #2

commanding the room
the hovering drone proclaims
to a dead planet

Herb Kauderer

tropical moon
colourful lizard preys
the quiet drizzle of rain

Kate Lisinska

Terran troop transport
downed by Martian separatists –
Phobos debris field

Lee Clark Zumpe

escape velocity—
leaving behind
another failed relationship

Lisa Timpf

Full Steam Ahead by Lisa Timpf

prospectors scuffle
sparking vicious range wars -
Saturn's lawless frontier

Lee Clark Zumpe

laser knife fight
the subtle scent of ozone
lingers in the air

Rick Jackofsky

AbracaDrabble
By Tyree Campbell

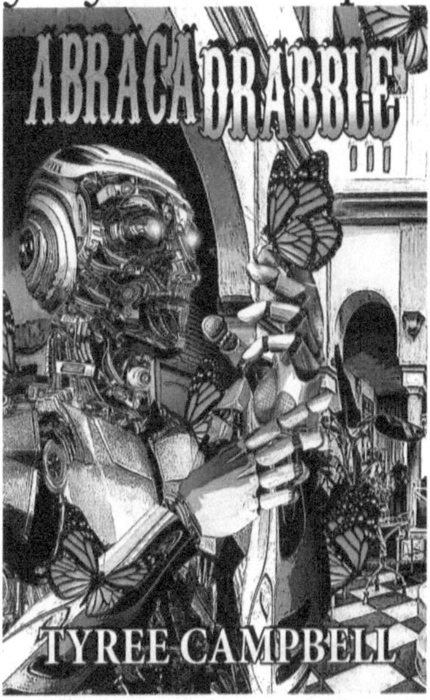
ABRACADRABBLE
TYREE CAMPBELL

A drabble is a story containing exactly 100 words. This volume contains drabbles with various science fiction and fantasy themes. In here you'll find trolls, time travel and outer space construction problems, courtesans who take instructions literally, dietary supplements, skip tracers, and demented nursery rhymes, and much more. Some are funny, some poignant, some serious, and some are all three.

Print ($8.00):
https://www.hiraethsffh.com/product-page/abracadrabble-by-tyree-campbell

PDF ($1.29):
https://www.hiraethsffh.com/product-page/abracadrabble-by-tyree-campbell-1

Postcards From Space

By Terrie Leigh Relf

Postcards from Space
Wish you were here
Terrie Leigh Relf

Here are some messages on postcards from space, found aboard a derelict craft that crashed on an arid, lifeless world. The OSPS (Outer Space Postal Service) has delivered these messages to Terrie, who now presents them to you. This is what it is like out there.

https://www.hiraethsffh.com/product-page/postcards-from-space-by-terrie-leigh-relf

first day of school
teacher with blue skin
alien invasion

Joy Yin

the low horizon
a rocking chair and soak tub
very rural Mars

Dylan Mabe

one ticket to go
a chance to be immortal
mamaw to the moon

Dylan Mabe

expectant robot
delivery date
factory stamped

Lauren McBride

intersecting
Martian phrases and Old Earth words
galactic crosswords

J.L. Sawyers

asking if items
can be beamed to Mars
cosmic customer service

J.L. Sawyers

deep-space drone descends
specs for cold-fusion tech
alien charity

Randall Andrews

bursts of magnetic color
auroras over
grand Ganymede's shore

Geoffrey Reiter

hoping climate change
accelerates
first earthlings on Mars

Douglas J. Lanzo

dental mishap
vampire faces centuries
of just blood pudding

Lee Strong, OFS

her guards know
all the hatchlings
have my eyes

David C. Kopaska-Merkel

"First Chill of Winter"

wife of ice man
arrested for attempted murder
do not touch the thermostat

Matthew Wilson

schrodiger's paradox
fearing results
do I buy cat food

Richard E Schell

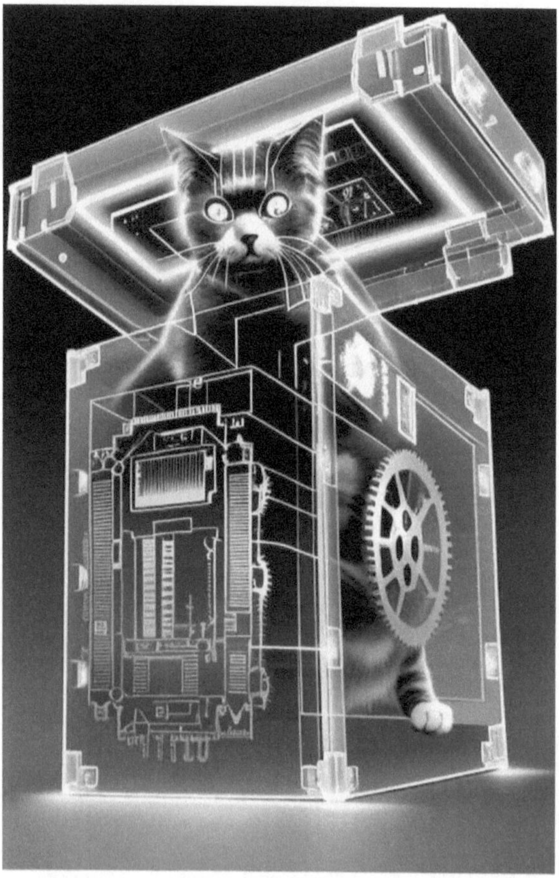

Steampunk Schrodiger's Cat
by Richard E. Schell

"Closest Satellite"

star-gazers looking up
at biggest supermoon for years
not seeing the coming werewolves

Matthew Wilson

"First Chill of Winter"

wife of ice man
arrested for attempted murder
do not touch the thermostat

Matthew Wilson

mycelium spreads
slowly consuming my flesh
winds carry my spores

Brian Barnett

casey jones coming through
ethereal train whistles cry
on time as always

Brian Barnett

my ex's head so hard to dust

David C. Kopaska-Merkel

Granddad's tomb
my turn to carry him
to the reunion

David C. Kopaska-Merkel

a pair of clackers
dangling from a length of string
your frozen eyeballs

Marcie Lynn Tentchoff

daisy blooms
on a hill of
human remains

Joy Yin

despite some warnings
he started the new device
and

Lee Strong, OFS

Living Bad Dreams

Denise Hatfield

LIVING BAD
DREAMS
DENISE
HATFIELD

When dreams come alive, there's no telling where they will lead. Everything changes when you realize that, dream or no dream, you're going to die. What do you do then?

Ordering Link:
Print Edition ($9.00):
https://www.hiraethsffh.com/product-page/living-bad-dreams-by-denise-hatfield-1
ePub Edition ($2.99):
https://www.hiraethsffh.com/product-page/living-bad-dreams-by-denise-hatfield-2
PDF Edition ($2.99):
https://www.hiraethsffh.com/product-page/living-bad-dreams-by-denise-hatfield

TANKA

I wish upon a distant star
called by those who dwell on
its only orbiting planet
hosting sentient life
the sun

John J. Dunphy

astronaut ape
from the failed planet Earth
feeling dismay
the beings on Planet X
look exactly like him

Elaine Dillof

hurtling through space
in a rocket
caterpillar feeling itself morph
something fabulist emerges
that could exist on the moon

Elaine Dillof

in pleasant Percival
I pole the barge toward shore
recreated Venice
without crowded city roar
spendy Martian tourist trap

Rebecca Olson

against solar winds

kids in escape pods
parents hold ship together
just long enough
the new world's gene pool expands
by two newly orphaned flowers

Herb Kauderer

on a planet
that's not Earth
a bird
that's not a sparrow
pecks at my face shield

Rick Jackofsky

lost with failing hope
our derelict craft adrift
distant beacon calls
unknown salvation
or a dream

Richard E Schell

Cosmic Entanglement
by Richard E. Schell

even we vampires
blanche at mocking winter sprites
a cruel sudden chill
drops of water beading on
my once warm goblet of blood

Marcie Lynn Tentchoff

erogenous zones
forbidden to touch
this interstellar dust
clings to every hollow
of your alien landscape

Julie Bloss Kelsey

SCIFAIKU ONE-BREATH

he smiled mechanically   positronic brain

Lauren McBride

OTHER FORMS (including: Sijo, Fibonacci, Cinquain, Minutes, Diminuendo, Ghazals,Threesomes, Brick, etc.)

SESTET

A Sestet

worm hole travel
we arrive
at our destination
before our youngest
can ask even once
'are we there yet?'

John J. Dunphy

CHERITA

we lost you during a snow white gale

ages passed and faded our immortal dreams
while we wandered and mourned our sibling

in time, mankind's blunders warmed the earth
and glaciers melted, flowing with our tears
to set you free once more

Marcie Lynn Tentchoff

GOGYOHKA

having loved
and lost
difficult to avoid you now
no matter how big
the starship

Lauren McBride

wondering
what she sees
in me
my alien lover
those compound eyes

Lauren McBride

unscripted

she thought she was abducted by aliens
but then they claimed to be time travellers
returned to refresh the gene pool
it was only after the probes were done
she realized she was just a reality show for the
future

Herb Kauderer

FIBONACCI

breathing easier

all
the
spacers
gather in
auditorium
waiting to meet new colony
mayor. this one has
promised an
increase
in
air

Herb Kauderer

FIBONACCI

huge
space
creature
devours an
entire tavern,
thought it was
Milky
Way
bar

Guy Belleranti

JOINED POEMS

(incl. renku and sedoka, joined fib. Etc.,)

Planetfail

Ann K. Schwader and David C. Kopaska-Merkel

spring sandstorm
outside the hab dome
a distant howl

planetary survey
missed something big

coyote dream
the single moon
I knew

secrets
of the dancing trees
skin crawls

windless rhythm
lifting our arms

sniffing
strange meat
the echoing sky

Radioactive Mars Haiku

Faint signs in the soil
Show near the end
Radioactive planet Mars

A buried sky dome
Top four inches above ground
Contains Martian bones

Underneath mars
Deep caverns with water
Mutated survive

Denny E. Marshall

Mars Haiku

Martians find new home
On one of the many planets
In Jupiter's core

Meteorite storms
Destroy all of the pyramids
On planet mars

Final group enters
Portal to varies worlds
Mars now deserted

Denny E. Marshall

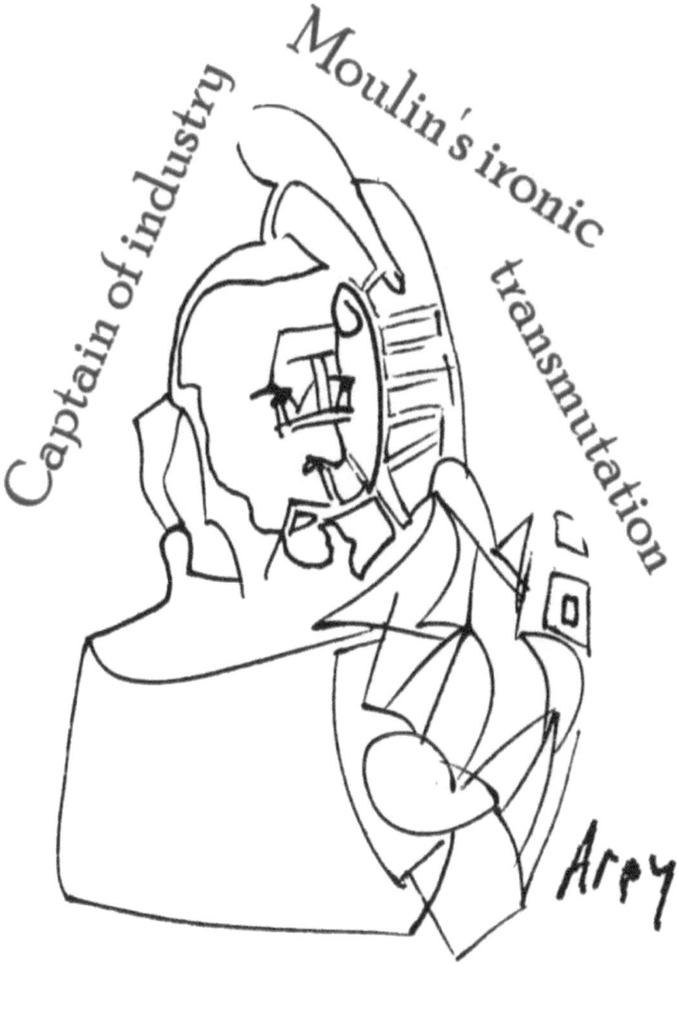
Captain of industry
Moulin's ironic
transmutation
Arey

I
wake
eager
to scare the
monster who enjoys
giving scares,
and I
do
give
it a
monster scare
for I have returned
after it
scared me
to
death

Guy Belleranti

Bucket List
Lisa Timpf

dwarfed by towering stones—
sunrise
at Stonehenge

castle ruins
on the ridge—
cruising the Rhine

colors dance
a heavenly ballet—
Northern Lights

VR Sim Session—
breezing through
our bucket list

Time Travel Triumphs
and Tribulations
Lisa Timpf

first kiss—
the magic
never fades

returning to pat
her favorite dog
over and rover

Do I know you from somewhere?—
always repeating
the same mistakes

changing the past—
how will we know
what we're missing?

Cats and Dogs in Space

Lisa Timpf

Cats and Dogs
in Space
Lisa Timpf

Cats in lab coats, running experiments on *us*. Robot dogs roaming Mars. Space-faring canines who mistake alien vessels for fetch toys. There are just some of the images you'll find in here. With inspiration from myths, news stories, nursery rhymes, personal experience, and a lifelong interest in science fiction, the poems are written in a variety of styles for your reading enjoyment. Reaching from the distant past to the far future, and points in between, *Cats and Dogs in Space* invites you to have some fun re-imagining man's best friend—and whatever it is that cats call themselves.

When we beamed the book to the future, here's what readers had to say:
"Purrfectly delightful! Enjoyable for readers of any stripe. Some of these poems are enough to make a cat laugh!" *Festus, ship's cat aboard the Silver Starr Spaceliner Frederika.*

"Meaty as a prime rib bone, and just as much fun to chew on! I'd give it two thumbs up—if I had opposable thumbs . . . " *Pepper, K-9 Operative, Galactic Space Services*

So there you have it! Get *your* claws on a copy today!

Print: www.hiraethsffh.com/product-page/cats-and-dogs-in-space-by-lisa-timpf

ePub: www.hiraethsffh.com/product-page/cats-and-dogs-in-space-by-lisa-timpf-2

HAIBUN and DRABBUN

HAIBUN
Grampa on Mars
Rebecca Olson

Grandpa was obsessed with Mars. His wallscreen always played photos, videos, or live streams of the Red Planet. So when he was getting on, it came as no surprise that he talked about going there and dying on Mars.

Of course, the tour company nixed his plans; he couldn't pass their medical exam to make the trip. Later that year, I went in his stead, with a bit of ash hidden in my personal allowance. Then just let it loose, to swirl in the slight breeze, home at last.

west Texas red dust
windswept land beneath pink sky
imagining Mars

The Train Always Goes Forward
Herb Kauderer

The memory of snow cannot be displaced by Martian duststorms. Tonia remembers the coziness of hot chocolate after shoveling out the van. The EVA suits are not so different from bundling up warm against a northern winter, but shoveling sand and dust out of the airlocks, and off the train tracks, is far more thankless than shoveling snow. And she recalls the way that bright winter sunshine melted some snow, and made the leavings stick together for easy tossing, and even a snowball fight.

Alone in her room, she showers away her sweat, and imagines an open window. All her reminiscing avoids the images of Carol, and the inspiration for her emigration. Being alone so far away is the solace that allowed her to move forward with her life. She is determined to do the next thing.

> she strives forward
> ignoring invisible
> chains that pull her back

DRABBUN
Malicious
Randall Andrews

We couldn't be sure of the aliens' intentions at first. Their massive mother ship hovered quietly in orbit for weeks following its arrival, offering no clues from which we could draw conclusions.

When the thousands of smaller ships deployed and descended across the globe, we got nervous but still hesitated to pass judgement. Even when one of them made a low pass over my fields, dropping what appeared to be a rain of pea-sized hail, I held out hope.

But now that those hungry buggers have
hatched and are laying waste to my crops . . .

invasive species
biological weapon
malicious intent

ARTICLE

Things As They Are: Digging at The Root of Horror and Scifaiku
By Robert E. Porter

Picture this:
Mother Goose and her wicked stepchildren heading down to the Thames riverbank. There, they make their deposits -- if not amends. Meanwhile, out on the water, the reverends Duckworth and Charles "Dodo" Dodgson paddle Liddell girls about. When it begins to rain, they rush for shore and shelter. This inspires "Dodo," who tells the story of Alice underground.

Edward Lear's career also took off with water-fouling waterfowl and other bird-brains. Painting wings on the plains for a lark, etc. Coincidence? Or caricature? Perhaps both? Oh, Bother!
"Victorian nonsense," said Adam Gopnik, "showed that parody can be a vehicle for the renewal of feeling." (Gopnik)

As if Victorians had been numb above their ankles before the Mad Tea Party, where--

"Alice sighed wearily. 'I think you might do something better with the time,' she said, 'than waste it in asking riddles that have no answers.'" (Carroll)

How timeless and true!

Speaking of riddles...

Dodgson saw his "barbershop" paradox published in the Mind of 1894. A decade later, Mad-Hatter-lookalike Bertrand Russell snatched it up. He tried to work it out in a book on mathematical principles. Russell had his own paradoxical barber, of course. The man's beard, like Schrodinger's filthy cat, muddied the waters of what could and could not be. But... Why impose the rigor mortis of logic on a living language?

What are "sense" and "nonsense" anyway? "Landmines," said Nina Lyon, "in a battle over logic's ability to untether truth from thought." (Lyon) Lyon should know, in the main. She studied "Snark" at Cardiff University in Wales. What a Job-like job! Most of us, being immersed, swim in our own local language. It is all we know, really. That Australian crawl has sunk into muscle memory. Tease a wave from the water? No way! We pull through. When presented with a self-contradictory statement ("I am lying," for ex.) or some other nonsense, we don't breakdown like the robots of vintage SF. ("Does not compute, does not compute..." Kaput! Steam from their ears and eyes glazed over.) No, we show our humanity with a Chesterton-like belly laugh or a Cheshire smile. Human behavior, after all, doesn't have to make sense. Nonsense is one of many "quantum" packets – with postage due -- that make up humanity.

Russell lifted the premises of mathematics and tried to put them on more logical footing. This work made sense to him, at least. He also taught a young Ludwig Wittgenstein. Hairy "Mad King" Ludwig would go on to shake the pillars of logic and language in the 20th century.

"Wittgenstein may well be the greatest philosopher that this century has yet seen," said David Pears, "but even those who make this claim for him find it hard to explain his message." (Pears, IX)

And no wonder--

"Less well-known," said Eric Gerlach, "is that Alice's Adventures in Wonderland was one of Wittgenstein's favorite books in English, for him a logician's catalog of the ways language can be misused." (Gerlach)

Hardly true! Language users define its usage. It's a democracy with universal suffrage. The foreign-born logician has no more say than a home-grown nose-picker, pickpocket, or pigs' feet pickler.

"Classical philosophy had failed to explain the world we lived in or the life we lived in it," said lecturer Paul Strathern. "If anything, it had only made matters worse. In attempting to analyze our common experience it had simply made it incomprehensible." (Strathern, 34)

An overgeneralization. Cliques, cults, and quacks have dissembled and mystified since the origin of language. The best of the world's philosophies, however. has always dealt with practical matters. For ex., how we should live out our lives and face the inevitable. Death, taxes, etc. Making room for childish nonsense, even.

Lewis Carroll told Alice to entertain, if not enlighten. Logic applied to language literally produced fantasy. How could anyone believe this stuff? And yet...

Another fable landed its moralist in hot water:

"If I were to suggest," said Bertrand Russell, "that between the Earth and Mars there is a china teapot revolving about the sun in an elliptical orbit, nobody would be able to disprove my assertion provided I were careful to add that the teapot is too small to be revealed even by our most powerful telescopes. But if I were to go on to say that, since my assertion cannot be disproved, it is an intolerable presumption on the part of human reason to doubt it, I should rightly be thought to be talking nonsense." (Russell)

There's that word again.

Edward Lear played with nonsense. It's a shame to ignore his real life's work, which was for the birds. There, he made nothing but sense. Compare his naturalist paintings to those of Audubon, for ex. His attention to detail subsequently broke the windows of his soul. As his eyeglasses thickened, he focused on bigger pictures. Lear traveled far and wide, landscape-painting for the batmen and Robin Hoods back home in merry England.

"Lear's verse also reflects the naturalist's turn of mind," according to Adam Gopnik. "If Carroll's nonsense satirizes the rise of philosophical idealism and the university, mocking people who think for a living and end up with absurd results, Lear's is a mockery of Victorian natural science, particularly the life sciences. Taxonomy, naming new species, domesticating the wild—that's the ground of his joking." (Gopnik)

How I doubt that! Dodgson and Lear ran circles around their critics, I think. But they're funny when they dig at what's true.

How like the "aha!" unearthed by horror or scifaiku.

WORKS CITED

Gerlach, Eric. "When Alice, Wittgenstein, and Russell met at the Mad Hatters Tea Party." The Philosopher, 1 September 2015. Online.

Gopnik, Adam. "Knowing Mr. Lear." New Yorker, 23 April 2018.

Lyon, Nina. "Slaying the Snark: what nonsense verse tells us about reality." Aeon, 3 January 2019. Online.

Pears, David. Ludwig Wittgenstein. Harvard University Press, 1986.

Russell, Bertrand. The Collected Papers of Bertrand Russell, Volume 11: Last Philosophical Testament, 1943-68, ed. John G. Slater and Peter Köllner. London: Routledge, 1997.

FEATURED POET:
Royal Baysinger

Venusian spiders
spin their webs
the muffled screams of space cadets

orders are orders
the starving crew
eats their stalwart captain

the final twists
of the bomb shelter's door lock...
a whippoorwill's cry

building robots
programmed
to build more robots

ending their date
in a moonlit park...
police tape off the area

burying our friend in sand
his disappearance
ruled a suicide

Trier 1580 —
the coven's runes
predict a bright future

browsing a brochure
of interstellar getaways
looking for your next escape velocity

dad lectures us the whole way there...
returning our pet
to its home planet

she reconstructs her face
this year
martian eyes are all the rage

he tells her it's love...
an automatic turn off
in the sex robot's programming

all alone —
closing the glassy eyes
of her stillborn android

getting a divorce
after the surgery
my artificial heart
longing
for other cyborgs

my ex turns the kids against me
— their family trip
to the re-memory clinic

Royal Baysinger lived most of his life on a small farm in Arizona before moving to Germany, then Canada. He has an MA in German and is currently living in Quebec where he is slowly learning French from his supportive wife and son. His short fiction and poetry have appeared in several publications as well as collected in anthology.

Royal Baysinger writes across many forms and genres. In addition to his speculative poetry featured previously in Dreams & Nightmares, Star*Line, Otoroshi and the Dwarf Stars Anthology, he has been widely published in most of the world's major English-language haiku journals and anthologies: Frogpond, Modern Haiku, and The Red Moon Anthology, among others. He recently received two Sakura Awards in the 2024 Vancouver Cherry Blossom Festival Haiku Invitational. His short fiction has also appeared in several publications, including a picture book, Kasanova — Lost in Love. You can follow him online at royalbaysinger.com or on Twitter/X @royalbaysinger.

INTERVIEW WITH FEATURED POET
Royal Baysinger

How long have you been writing poetry?

I began writing and performing poetry at age 10, but once I became a teenager, I found other interests. A few lines found their way into sketchbooks I kept over the years, but I didn't start writing and submitting poetry until 2022.

Did you begin writing haiku before you branched out to scifaiku?

Yes, I did. I had been writing haiku for almost a year before I discovered the term "scifaiku" while doing some research on its related forms. And it hooked me immediately.

Where did you learn to write scifaiku?

Studying and writing haiku gives you all the tools you need to write effective scifaiku. That, and a love for the speculative genre, of course.

Whose poetry has influenced you the most?

In haiku, there are two poets in particular who have influenced me the most. Deborah A. Bennett does incredible work weaving lyrical poetry again and again into tiny spaces. And Ben Gaa is a true modern master of the form. He always has such vivid scenes that make me feel like I'm reading one of the classical Japanese poets.

Who is your favorite poet?

Impossible to list just one. There are the obvious: Shakespeare and Goethe, Dickinson and Frost. As well as so many others from days gone by. But for more modern fair, Ocean Vuong's "Aubade with Burning City" is one of the most electric pieces of poetry I've ever experienced. And though I've only read her picture books so far, Jacqueline Woodson just has a way with words! I look forward to reading more of her.

What/who is your main inspiration?

For speculative work, Ray Bradbury and Rod Serling stand out as major inspirations. Their character work, world-building, and tension, all contained within the short story space, really are unparalleled.

What poetry magazines do you read/contribute to?

*There are so many fantastic haiku and short form magazines I am proud to be a part of: Scifaikuest (obviously), Dreams & Nightmares, Star*Line, Frogpond, Modern Haiku, Ribbons, The Heron's Nest, Mayfly, First Frost, Acorn, Kokako, Presence, Noon, Hedgerow, Haiku Canada Review, cattails, The Mamba Journal, Wales Haiku Journal, Akitsu Quarterly, Seashores, Poetry Pea, and bottle rockets.*

There are plenty of other magazines I follow and look forward to contributing to one day, including Rattle and Fantasy & Science Fiction.

I'm just getting started.

FAVORITE POEM by editor, t. santitoro

the plunger sinks
torpor spreads beneath his skin
with dreams of her

Christina Nordlander
What a Valentine!

-OR-

her guards know
all the hatchlings
have my eyes
SO many things going on here!
Wonderful show-don't-tell moment!

David C. Kopaska-Merkel

-OR-

erogenous zones
forbidden to touch
this interstellar dust
clings to every hollow
of your alien landscape

Julie Bloss Kelsey
Excellent double entendres!

-OR-

ending their date
in a moonlit park...
police tape off the area

Royal Baysinger
SO concise and packs a powerful punch!

Once again, I'm stymied! I told you in the beginning that we had some excellent material in this issue, and I wasn't kidding. I'm leaving this one to YOU! Which is your favorite????
--t. santitoro, editor

www.ingramcontent.com/pod-product-compliance
Lightning Source LLC
LaVergne TN
LVHW092059060526
838201LV00047B/1472
* 9 7 9 8 3 4 8 4 9 3 1 5 8 *